# The American Flag

Tristan Boyer Binns

Heinemann Library
Chicago, Illinois

© 2001 Reed Educational & Professional Publishing
Published by Heinemann Library,
an imprint of Reed Educational & Professional Publishing,
Chicago, IL

Customer Service  888-454-2279

Visit our website at www.heinemannlibrary.com

Designed by Lisa Buckley
Printed in U.S.A. by Lake Book Manufacturing

05 04
10 9 8 7 6

**Library of Congress Cataloging-in-Publication Data**
Binns, Tristan Boyer, 1968-
     The American flag / Tristan Boyer Binns.
          p. cm. -- (Symbols of freedom)
     Includes bibliographical references (p. ) and index.
     ISBN 1-58810-117-7 (lib. bdg)          ISBN 1-58810-401-X (pbk. bdg.)
       1. Flags--United States--History--Juvenile literature.  [1. Flags--United States--History.]
     I. Title.

CR113 .B53 2001
929.9'0973--dc21
                                                                    00-058146

**Acknowledgments**
The author and publishers are grateful to the following for permission to reproduce copyright material: p.4 George Lepp/Corbis, p.5 David Burnett/Contact Press Images/PictureQuest, p.6 Adam Woolfitt/Corbis, p.7 Rodger Ressmeyer/NASA/Corbis, p.8 Michael Brosilow, p.9 Kevin Flemming/Corbis, p.10, 13 Joseph Sohm/ChromoSohm Inc./Corbis, p.11 Bob Daemmrich/Stock, Boston/PictureQuest, p.12 Rick Browne/Stock, Boston/PictureQuest, p.14, 15, 22, 26, 27 Courtesy of Marie and Boelsaw Mastai, p.16 PictureQuest, p.17 Paul Errico/Courtesy of The City of Somerville MA, p.18 Bettemann/Corbis, p.19 Col. Louis H. Frohman/Corbis, p.20 Library of Congress, p.21 Robert Edge Pine/The Historical Society of Pennsylvannia [Accession #1891.7], p.23 Ed Jackson/Carl Vison Institute/ University of Georgia, p.24 National Park Service, p.25 Smithsonian Institution.
Cover photograph by Joseph Sohm/ChromoSohm Inc./Corbis.

Special thanks to the city of Somerville, MA.

Every effort has been made to contact copyright holders of any material reproduced in this book. Any omissions will be rectified in subsequent printings if notice is given to the publisher.

Some words are shown in bold, **like this.**
You can find out what they mean by looking in the glossary.

# Contents

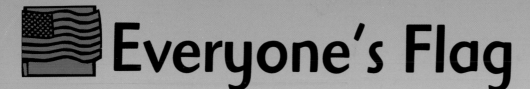 # Everyone's Flag

The American flag is red, white, and blue.
It has six white stripes and seven red stripes.
It has 50 white stars on a blue background.

The flag is an important **symbol.** It tells us we are all part of one country. People everywhere know that the flag stands for the United **States** of America.

# Flying the Flag

The flag flies outside most schools. It flies over the **White House** when the president is there. It flies outside government buildings, such as the post office.

The flag is shown on postage stamps. Soldiers, sailors, and astronauts wear the flag on their uniforms.

# At School and at Home

School children say the Pledge of Allegiance to the flag in their classrooms. The pledge puts the ideas of the flag into words. It says that we believe in **liberty** and **justice** for everyone.

Many people fly the flag at their homes. Flying the flag is a way people can show love and respect for their country.

# Respecting the Flag

People show respect for the flag by treating it with care. Only special **waterproof** flags may be flown outside in bad weather. The flag may not fly at night unless it is lit up.

The flag should not touch the ground. It should be raised up a flagpole quickly. It should be lowered slowly. There is a special way to fold the flag.

# Making Flags

Today, many people and companies make flags. There are rules about how American flags are made.

All American flags look the same. The red and white stripes are always in the same place. The stars always go in a blue square. There is always a red stripe at the top and the bottom.

# Flags for the Colonies

AN APPEAL TO HEAVEN

At first, the United **States** was just a small group of thirteen different **colonies.** Each colony wanted its own flag. Some colonies had flags with pine trees on them.

DONT TREAD ON ME

Other colonies had flags with rattlesnakes on them. These **symbols** meant different things. A pine tree meant that the colony was strong. A snake meant danger.

# The First American Flag

The **colonies** joined together. They would fight a war to become **independent** from **Britain.** The **colonists** decided on one flag to show that they were all working together.

The Grand Union flag had thirteen stripes
and a small **British** flag in the corner.
George Washington first flew it during
a battle with British soldiers in 1776.

# The Stars and Stripes

On July 4, 1776 the United **States** became an **independent** country. **Congress** called for a new flag. It was called the "Stars and Stripes."

The **colonies** were now states. So the new flag still had thirteen stripes. But the **British** flag was gone. Instead, there were thirteen white stars on a blue square, one for each state.

# Who Made the Flag?

There is a story that Betsy Ross may have sewed the first Stars and Stripes. She was a **seamstress** in Philadelphia. She may have helped George Washington design the flag.

A man named Francis Hopkinson was probably the real designer of the Stars and Stripes. He was a lawyer, a musician, and a judge. He **represented** the **state** of New Jersey in **Congress.**

21

# How Flags Looked

People sewed the first flags by hand. There were no laws to say how the stars should look. Some people even added extra stars!

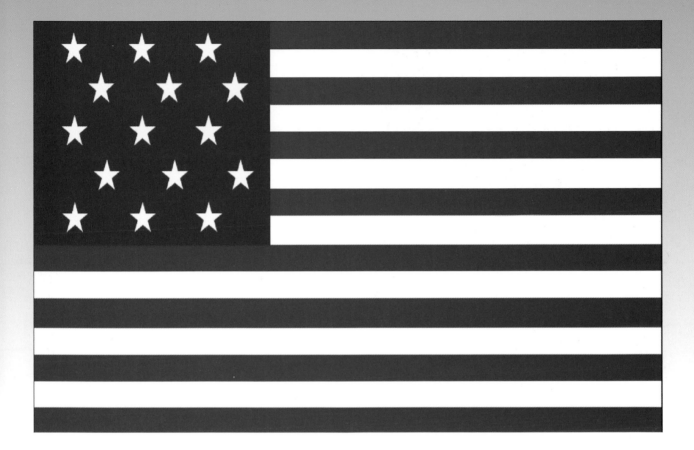

Then, Kentucky and Vermont joined the United **States.** The design of the flag was changed to fifteen stars and fifteen stripes. The flag looked this way for many years.

# ⚑ Sign of Victory

In 1814, **Britain** and the United **States** were at war again. One night, **Francis Scott Key** watched as the **British** fired on Fort McHenry, Maryland. Could the fort hold out through the night?

The sun rose. The flag was still there! The United States had won. Francis Scott Key wrote a poem called "The Star-Spangled Banner." It became our **national anthem.**

# More New States

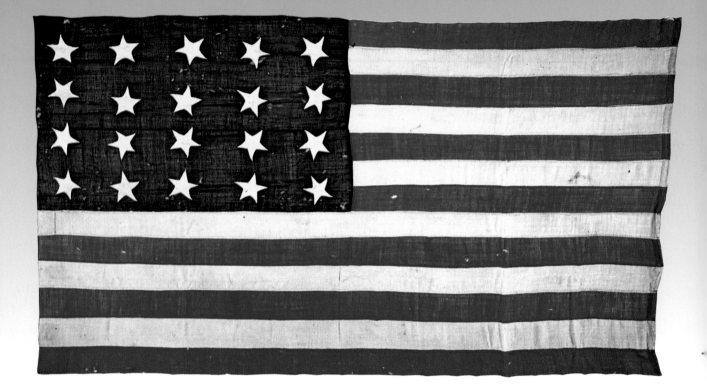

As time went on, there were more and more **states. Congress** decided to stop adding stripes for each new state.

A new law said that each state would have a star. But there would only be thirteen stripes, one for each of the original thirteen states.

# The Flag on the Move

GEOGRAPHIC
SOUTH POLE

ROALD AMUNDSEN — ROBERT F. SCOTT
DECEMBER 14, 1911 — JANUARY 17, 1912

"So we arrived and were able to plant our flag at the geographical South Pole."

"The Pole. Yes, but under very different circumstances from those expected."

ELEVATION 9,301 FT.

The flag has been many places! It was taken to the North Pole almost 100 years ago. It was dropped onto the South Pole from an airplane about 70 years ago.

It was carried to the top of **Mount Everest** about 40 years ago. It was planted on the Moon about 30 years ago.

# Fact File

# American Flag

★ The biggest flag weighs as much as a large horse.

★ Each star is as tall as a man, and each stripe is as tall as the ceiling in a house!

★ The colors of the flag have meanings:

★Red means **courage**

★White means goodness

★Blue means **justice**

★ People call our flag:

*The Stars and Stripes*        *The Star-Spangled Banner*

*Old Glory*                            *The Starry Flag*

*The Stars and Bars*            *Freedom's Banner*